This journal belongs to:

_____

&

_____

OUR DAILY QUESTION

All Scripture quotations are taken from the Holy Bible, New International Version®, NIV® Copyright © 1973, 1978, 1984, 2011 by Biblica, Inc.® Used by permission. All rights reserved worldwide.

Hardcover ISBN 978-0-593-19293-1

Design by Nicole Block
Illustrations by frescomovie/Shutterstock.com

Published in the United States by Ink & Willow, an imprint of Random House, a division of Penguin Random House LLC.

INK & WILLOW and its colophon are trademarks of Penguin Random House LLC.

Printed in China

2020—First Edition

10 9 8 7 6 5 4 3 2 1

SPECIAL SALES
Most Ink & Willow books are available at special quantity discounts when purchased in bulk by corporations, organizations, and special-interest groups. Custom imprinting or excerpting can also be done to fit special needs. For information, please e-mail specialmarketscms@penguinrandomhouse.com.

Our

Daily
Question

A Three-Year Journal for Couples

Ink &
Willow

Welcome to Your Story!

Be completely humble and gentle;
be patient, bearing with one another in love.
Make every effort to keep the unity of the
Spirit through the bond of peace.

Ephesians 4:2–3

LIFE GOES QUICKLY. While we're all rushing furiously to pursue our dreams of a successful career, a happy family, and a healthy body, or to get to that ineffable place of feeling as though *we've made it*, we can often miss the most precious and priceless moments that occur every day.

This journal is designed to help you and your significant other stop and notice those small moments so that you can look back and see your evolution as individuals and as a couple. For the next three years, you'll embark on a daily journey to claim a few quiet moments and reflect on your life together. Some prompts might tease out your quirky side or spark friendly debate about who has better taste in music, while others will prod you to explore how each of you tends to face challenges or how you experience God and spirituality.

By responding to the prompts on these pages, together you'll create a beautiful and wholly unique encapsulation of who you are in that moment and the ways you grew over the course of three years. Simply enter the current year in the space provided and answer one question every day—one of you responds on the gray lines and the other on the gold lines. No matter how you approach this daily practice, we hope that the three-year journey you take prompts new discussions, invites deeper connection, and brings you closer together.

January

1
January

What is your New Year's resolution?

20___ _____

_____

_____

_____

_____

_____

20___ _____

_____

_____

_____

_____

_____

20___ _____

_____

_____

_____

_____

_____

What's something you remember about your first
year together?

2
January

20___ _____

_____

_____

_____

_____

20___ _____

_____

_____

_____

_____

20___ _____

_____

_____

_____

_____

3
January

If you could accomplish one thing this year as a couple, what would it be?

20___ _____

_____

_____

_____

_____

20___ _____

_____

_____

_____

_____

20___ _____

_____

_____

_____

_____

What would you consider your verse or quote
of the year?

4
January

20___ _____

_____

_____

_____

_____

20___ _____

_____

_____

_____

_____

20___ _____

_____

_____

_____

_____

5

January

What was one of your first impressions of your significant other?

20___ _____

_____

_____

_____

_____

20___ _____

_____

_____

_____

_____

20___ _____

_____

_____

_____

_____

If you could choose anyone, real or fictional, to act as your personal tour guide for a day, who would it be?

6
January

20___ _____

_____

_____

_____

_____

20___ _____

_____

_____

_____

_____

20___ _____

_____

_____

_____

_____

7

January

"I keep forgetting _____."

20___ _____

_____

_____

_____

_____

_____

20___ _____

_____

_____

_____

_____

_____

20___ _____

_____

_____

_____

_____

_____

If you were a couple in one of your favorite movies, which one would you be?

8
January

20____ _____

_____

_____

_____

_____

20____ _____

_____

_____

_____

_____

20____ _____

_____

_____

_____

_____

9
January

How does your significant other support you when you're facing a difficulty or challenge?

20___ ————————————————————————————

20___ ————————————————————————————

20___ ————————————————————————————

What is one thing you would do to survive the zombie apocalypse?

10
January

20___

20___

20___

11
January

What is something that matters to other people but doesn't matter to you?

20____ _____

_____

_____

_____

_____

20____ _____

_____

_____

_____

_____

20____ _____

_____

_____

_____

_____

What are your top three goals for this year?

12
January

20___ _____

_____

_____

_____

_____

20___ _____

_____

_____

_____

_____

20___ _____

_____

_____

_____

_____

13
January

What emotions do you feel when you look back at old photos of you as a couple?

20____ _____

_____

_____

_____

_____

_____

20____ _____

_____

_____

_____

_____

_____

20____ _____

_____

_____

_____

_____

_____

If you were to focus on one word for this year, what would it be?

14
January

20___ _____

_____

_____

_____

_____

20___ _____

_____

_____

_____

_____

20___ _____

_____

_____

_____

_____

15
January

What is one trick you would like to teach your
pet or a friend's pet?

20_____ _____

_____

_____

_____

_____

20_____ _____

_____

_____

_____

_____

20_____ _____

_____

_____

_____

_____

What hobby do you like doing together?

18
January

20___ _____

_____

_____

_____

_____

20___ _____

_____

_____

_____

_____

20___ _____

_____

_____

_____

_____

19
January

If you could spend the night in any museum,
which one would you pick?

20____ _____

_____

_____

_____

_____

20____ _____

_____

_____

_____

_____

20____ _____

_____

_____

_____

_____

What was your takeaway from a book you
recently read?

20
January

20____ _____

_____

_____

_____

_____

_____

20____ _____

_____

_____

_____

_____

_____

20____ _____

_____

_____

_____

_____

_____

21
January

What is your current approach to conflict?

20___ _____

_____

_____

_____

_____

20___ _____

_____

_____

_____

_____

20___ _____

_____

_____

_____

_____

Where do you want to travel in the coming year?

22
January

20____ _____

_____

_____

_____

_____

_____

20____ _____

_____

_____

_____

_____

_____

20____ _____

_____

_____

_____

_____

_____

23
January

How can your significant other help you grow deeper in your faith?

20___ _____

_____

_____

_____

_____

20___ _____

_____

_____

_____

_____

20___ _____

_____

_____

_____

_____

If you received one hundred dollars as a gift, how would you spend it? How about one thousand dollars?

24
January

20_____ _____

_____

_____

_____

_____

_____

20_____ _____

_____

_____

_____

_____

_____

20_____ _____

_____

_____

_____

_____

_____

25
January

What makes you feel loved and respected in your relationship?

20___ _____

_____

_____

_____

_____

20___ _____

_____

_____

_____

_____

20___ _____

_____

_____

_____

_____

If you were an Olympic athlete, in which sport would you want to compete?

26
January

20___ _____

_____

_____

_____

_____

20___ _____

_____

_____

_____

_____

20___ _____

_____

_____

_____

_____

27
January

What's one thing that made you realize you wanted to have a future together with your partner?

20_____ _____

_____

_____

_____

_____

20_____ _____

_____

_____

_____

_____

20_____ _____

_____

_____

_____

_____

What's a childhood story you'll never forget?

28
January

20_____ _____

_____

_____

_____

_____

20_____ _____

_____

_____

_____

_____

20_____ _____

_____

_____

_____

_____

29
January

What brings you the most joy in your current job?

20___ —————————————————————————

————————————————————————————————

————————————————————————————————

————————————————————————————————

————————————————————————————————

20___ —————————————————————————

————————————————————————————————

————————————————————————————————

————————————————————————————————

————————————————————————————————

20___ —————————————————————————

————————————————————————————————

————————————————————————————————

————————————————————————————————

————————————————————————————————

Who or what was in the last photograph you took?

30
January

20___ _____

_____

_____

_____

_____

_____

20___ _____

_____

_____

_____

_____

_____

20___ _____

_____

_____

_____

_____

_____

31
January

What do you hope to accomplish in the next six months?

20____ _____

_____

_____

_____

_____

_____

20____ _____

_____

_____

_____

_____

_____

20____ _____

_____

_____

_____

_____

_____

February

1
February

If you could have a nontraditional pet, what would it be?

20_____

20_____

20_____

What is a current motto or piece of advice
you live by?

2
February

20___ _____

_____

_____

_____

_____

20___ _____

_____

_____

_____

_____

20___ _____

_____

_____

_____

_____

3
February

What is one trait you inherited from either of your parents?

20____ _____

_____

_____

_____

_____

20____ _____

_____

_____

_____

_____

20____ _____

_____

_____

_____

_____

What simple gesture would make your day?

4
February

20___ _____

_____

_____

_____

_____

20___ _____

_____

_____

_____

_____

20___ _____

_____

_____

_____

_____

5
February

What is your favorite restaurant to visit together?
On your own?

20____ _____

_____

_____

_____

_____

20____ _____

_____

_____

_____

_____

20____ _____

_____

_____

_____

_____

If you could have the skill of any one musician, who would it be?

6
February

20___ _____

_____

_____

_____

_____

20___ _____

_____

_____

_____

_____

20___ _____

_____

_____

_____

_____

7
February

What is the last book you read?

20_____ _____

_____

_____

_____

_____

20_____ _____

_____

_____

_____

_____

20_____ _____

_____

_____

_____

_____

What is one thing you think is hard about being in a relationship?

8
February

20____ _____

20____ _____

20____ _____

9
February

If you had only one day to live, how would you spend it?

20___ _____

_____

_____

_____

_____

20___ _____

_____

_____

_____

_____

20___ _____

_____

_____

_____

_____

Would you rather travel to the future or the past? Why?

10
February

20___ _____

_____

_____

_____

_____

20___ _____

_____

_____

_____

_____

20___ _____

_____

_____

_____

_____

11
February

Describe an event that shaped who you are today.

20_____ _____

_____

_____

_____

_____

20_____ _____

_____

_____

_____

_____

20_____ _____

_____

_____

_____

_____

If you could ask God any question right now and get a definitive answer, what would it be?

12
February

20____ _____

_____

_____

_____

_____

20____ _____

_____

_____

_____

_____

20____ _____

_____

_____

_____

_____

13
February

"I wish I had more time to _____."

20___ _____

_____

_____

_____

_____

20___ _____

_____

_____

_____

_____

20___ _____

_____

_____

_____

_____

How did you spend Valentine's Day?

14
February

20____ _____

_____

_____

_____

_____

_____

20____ _____

_____

_____

_____

_____

_____

20____ _____

_____

_____

_____

_____

_____

15
February

How did you experience love in the past year?

20___ _____

_____

_____

_____

_____

_____

20___ _____

_____

_____

_____

_____

_____

20___ _____

_____

_____

_____

_____

_____

When was the last time you laughed out loud?

16
February

20___ _____

_____

_____

_____

_____

20___ _____

_____

_____

_____

_____

20___ _____

_____

_____

_____

_____

17
February

What story do you want to make sure you pass on to future generations?

20____

20____

20____

"I'm worried about _____."

20___ _____

_____

_____

_____

_____

_____

20___ _____

_____

_____

_____

_____

_____

20___ _____

_____

_____

_____

_____

_____

19
February

What is one fun feature your dream house would have?

20___ _____

_____

_____

_____

_____

20___ _____

_____

_____

_____

_____

20___ _____

_____

_____

_____

_____

Describe a moment in your life when you
felt invincible.

20
February

20_____ _____

_____

_____

_____

_____

_____

20_____ _____

_____

_____

_____

_____

_____

20_____ _____

_____

_____

_____

_____

_____

21
February

Who is someone you can lean on for
relationship advice?

20____ _____

_____

_____

_____

_____

20____ _____

_____

_____

_____

_____

20____ _____

_____

_____

_____

_____

If you got a new pet today, what would you name it?

22
February

20___ _____

_____

_____

_____

_____

20___ _____

_____

_____

_____

_____

20___ _____

_____

_____

_____

_____

23
February

What's your current favorite song?

20_____ _____

_____

_____

_____

_____

20_____ _____

_____

_____

_____

_____

20_____ _____

_____

_____

_____

_____

Describe a memorable gift you received as a child.

24
February

20___ _____

_____

_____

_____

_____

20___ _____

_____

_____

_____

_____

20___ _____

_____

_____

_____

_____

25
February

If you could become an expert at one skill, what would it be?

20___ _____

_____

_____

_____

_____

20___ _____

_____

_____

_____

_____

20___ _____

_____

_____

_____

_____

What is something you did with your childhood
friends that seems ridiculous now?

26
February

20___ _____

_____

_____

_____

_____

20___ _____

_____

_____

_____

_____

20___ _____

_____

_____

_____

_____

27
February

What's one habit you know you should probably break?

20_____ _____

_____

_____

_____

_____

20_____ _____

_____

_____

_____

_____

20_____ _____

_____

_____

_____

_____

What verse or quote has recently offered you the most comfort during hardship?

28
February

20____ _____

_____

_____

_____

_____

20____ _____

_____

_____

_____

_____

20____ _____

_____

_____

_____

_____

29
February

If you could create a fictional family using characters from books, TV shows, or movies, who would your parents be? Your siblings? In-laws?

20_____ _____

_____

_____

_____

_____

_____

20_____ _____

_____

_____

_____

_____

_____

20_____ _____

_____

_____

_____

_____

_____

March

1
March

What is one daily practice you can implement to build each other up?

20___ _____

_____

_____

_____

_____

20___ _____

_____

_____

_____

_____

20___ _____

_____

_____

_____

_____

How do you think you have changed since you first met your significant other?

2
March

20___ _____

_____

_____

_____

_____

20___ _____

_____

_____

_____

_____

20___ _____

_____

_____

_____

_____

3
March

Describe a funny travel experience.

20___ _____

_____

_____

_____

_____

20___ _____

_____

_____

_____

_____

20___ _____

_____

_____

_____

_____

What has your partner done recently that you are proud of?

4
March

20___ _____

_____

_____

_____

_____

20___ _____

_____

_____

_____

_____

20___ _____

_____

_____

_____

_____

5
March

What is one pet name you have for your significant other that some might think is ridiculous?

20_____ _____

_____

_____

_____

_____

20_____ _____

_____

_____

_____

_____

20_____ _____

_____

_____

_____

_____

What's a childhood story your family never lets you forget?

6
March

20___ _____

_____

_____

_____

_____

20___ _____

_____

_____

_____

_____

20___ _____

_____

_____

_____

_____

7
March

What's the last thing that scared you?

20____ _____

_____

_____

_____

_____

20____ _____

_____

_____

_____

_____

20____ _____

_____

_____

_____

_____

What are you hoping to learn in the coming year?

8
March

20___ _____

_____

_____

_____

_____

20___ _____

_____

_____

_____

_____

20___ _____

_____

_____

_____

_____

9
March

What is something you remember about one of your "firsts" together (first date, kiss, anniversary, shared holiday, etc.)?

20____ _____

_____

_____

_____

_____

20____ _____

_____

_____

_____

_____

20____ _____

_____

_____

_____

_____

Other than your significant other, whom do you confide in?

10
March

20___ _____

_____

_____

_____

_____

20___ _____

_____

_____

_____

_____

20___ _____

_____

_____

_____

_____

11
March

What is the last thing that surprised you? Did you like it or not?

20____ _____

_____

_____

_____

_____

20____ _____

_____

_____

_____

_____

20____ _____

_____

_____

_____

_____

What is one profession you have dreamed
of having?

12
March

20____ _____

_____

_____

_____

_____

20____ _____

_____

_____

_____

_____

20____ _____

_____

_____

_____

_____

13
March

If you could perfectly capture on canvas a moment from your life together, which one would it be?

20____ _____

_____

_____

_____

_____

20____ _____

_____

_____

_____

_____

20____ _____

_____

_____

_____

_____

If you could spend a day with any fictional character, who would it be?

14
March

20____ _____

_____

_____

_____

_____

20____ _____

_____

_____

_____

_____

20____ _____

_____

_____

_____

_____

15
March

Describe a concern or problem you have resolved successfully in the past month.

20___ _____

_____

_____

_____

_____

20___ _____

_____

_____

_____

_____

20___ _____

_____

_____

_____

_____

Where do you feel most inspired?

16
March

20___ _____

_____

_____

_____

_____

20___ _____

_____

_____

_____

_____

20___ _____

_____

_____

_____

_____

17
March

What is something you always wanted to do as a child?

20_____

20_____

20_____

How can you make a daily habit of pursuing God together?

18
March

20___ _____

_____

_____

_____

_____

20___ _____

_____

_____

_____

_____

20___ _____

_____

_____

_____

_____

19
March

If you were in the witness protection program, what would be your new name and where would you want to go?

20____ _____

_____

_____

_____

_____

20____ _____

_____

_____

_____

_____

20____ _____

_____

_____

_____

_____

What is something your significant other does
better than you do?

20
March

20___ _____

_____

_____

_____

_____

20___ _____

_____

_____

_____

_____

20___ _____

_____

_____

_____

_____

23
March

What was the last compliment you received that you don't quite believe?

20____ _____

_____

_____

_____

_____

20____ _____

_____

_____

_____

_____

20____ _____

_____

_____

_____

_____

What is at the top of your bucket list right now?

24
March

20_____ _____

_____

_____

_____

_____

20_____ _____

_____

_____

_____

_____

20_____ _____

_____

_____

_____

_____

25
March

Write down a memorable piece of advice someone once gave you.

20____ _____

_____

_____

_____

_____

20____ _____

_____

_____

_____

_____

20____ _____

_____

_____

_____

_____

What activity do you enjoy doing with your pet? Or, if you don't have a pet, what activity *would* you enjoy doing?

26
March

20_____ _____

_____

_____

_____

_____

20_____ _____

_____

_____

_____

_____

20_____ _____

_____

_____

_____

_____

27
March

Would you rather have ten close friends or one best friend?

20___ _____

_____

_____

_____

_____

20___ _____

_____

_____

_____

_____

20___ _____

_____

_____

_____

_____

As you grow older, do you picture yourself living near or far away from family?

28
March

20___ _____

_____

_____

_____

_____

20___ _____

_____

_____

_____

_____

20___ _____

_____

_____

_____

_____

29
March

Name a specific way you can be generous with others this week.

20___ _____

_____

_____

_____

_____

20___ _____

_____

_____

_____

_____

20___ _____

_____

_____

_____

_____

Which of your significant other's hobbies or
interests are currently the most appealing to you?

30
March

20____ _____

_____

_____

_____

_____

20____ _____

_____

_____

_____

_____

20____ _____

_____

_____

_____

_____

31
March

If you had to pick a color to describe your current mood, which would you choose?

20___

20___

20___

April

1
April

When is the last time you got caught in the rain?

20___ _____

_____

_____

_____

_____

20___ _____

_____

_____

_____

_____

20___ _____

_____

_____

_____

_____

Which fictional character currently reminds you of your significant other?

2
April

20_____ _____

_____

_____

_____

_____

20_____ _____

_____

_____

_____

_____

20_____ _____

_____

_____

_____

_____

3
April

What is the hardest aspect of your job?

20___ _____

_____

_____

_____

_____

_____

20___ _____

_____

_____

_____

_____

_____

20___ _____

_____

_____

_____

_____

_____

How did you celebrate your last birthday?

4
April

20___ _____

_____

_____

_____

_____

20___ _____

_____

_____

_____

_____

20___ _____

_____

_____

_____

_____

5
April

What do you need prayer for right now?

20____ _____

_____

_____

_____

_____

20____ _____

_____

_____

_____

_____

20____ _____

_____

_____

_____

_____

If you could solve one world problem, which would it be?

6
April

20___ _____

_____

_____

_____

_____

20___ _____

_____

_____

_____

_____

20___ _____

_____

_____

_____

_____

7
April

Beach or mountains? Why?

20___ _____

_____

_____

_____

_____

20___ _____

_____

_____

_____

_____

20___ _____

_____

_____

_____

_____

"One current fad that I don't understand is
_____."

8
April

20___ _____
_____
_____
_____
_____
_____

20___ _____
_____
_____
_____
_____
_____

20___ _____
_____
_____
_____
_____
_____

9
April

How did the weather today affect your mood?

20____ _____

_____

_____

_____

_____

20____ _____

_____

_____

_____

_____

20____ _____

_____

_____

_____

_____

What inside joke do you remember sharing early in your relationship?

10
April

20___ _____

_____

_____

_____

_____

20___ _____

_____

_____

_____

_____

20___ _____

_____

_____

_____

_____

11
April

"I like it when my significant other wears
_____."

20___ _____

_____

_____

_____

_____

_____

20___ _____

_____

_____

_____

_____

_____

20___ _____

_____

_____

_____

_____

_____

What is one thing you'd like to change about your living space?

12
April

20___ _____

_____

_____

_____

_____

_____

20___ _____

_____

_____

_____

_____

_____

20___ _____

_____

_____

_____

_____

_____

13
April

What is a key difference between you and
your partner's relationship and your parents'
relationship?

20___ _____

_____

_____

_____

_____

20___ _____

_____

_____

_____

_____

20___ _____

_____

_____

_____

_____

Create a haiku (a poem of seventeen syllables, in three lines of five, seven, and five syllables) about your partner.

14
April

20___ _____

_____

_____

_____

_____

20___ _____

_____

_____

_____

_____

20___ _____

_____

_____

_____

_____

15
April

What do you currently enjoy doing in your free time?

20___ _____

_____

_____

_____

_____

_____

20___ _____

_____

_____

_____

_____

_____

20___ _____

_____

_____

_____

_____

_____

If you could meet any band, past or present, which one would it be?

16
April

20___ _____

_____

_____

_____

_____

20___ _____

_____

_____

_____

_____

20___ _____

_____

_____

_____

_____

17
April

How would you like to be able to express your feelings when you're sad, anxious, or upset?

20____

_____

_____

_____

_____

_____

20____

_____

_____

_____

_____

_____

20____

_____

_____

_____

_____

_____

What exotic food would you like to try?

22
April

20___ ___

20___ ___

20___ ___

23
April

If you were granted one do-over for something in the past year, how would you use it?

20___ _____

_____

_____

_____

_____

_____

20___ _____

_____

_____

_____

_____

_____

20___ _____

_____

_____

_____

_____

_____

What is one thing you think is funny that no one else does?

24
April

20____

_____

_____

_____

_____

_____

20____

_____

_____

_____

_____

_____

20____

_____

_____

_____

_____

_____

25
April

One of my favorite things about our family is
_____.

20___ _____

20___ _____

20___ _____

What do you think you and your partner's life together will look like in 5 years? In 10 years?

26
April

20____ _____

_____

_____

_____

_____

_____

20____ _____

_____

_____

_____

_____

_____

20____ _____

_____

_____

_____

_____

_____

27
April

When you were a child, what is something you learned from your best friend?

20____ _____

_____

_____

_____

_____

20____ _____

_____

_____

_____

_____

20____ _____

_____

_____

_____

_____

What small gift would you enjoy receiving on an ordinary day?

28
April

20___ _____

_____

_____

_____

_____

20___ _____

_____

_____

_____

_____

20___ _____

_____

_____

_____

_____

29
April

If you could play any professional sport, what would it be?

20_____ _____

_____

_____

_____

_____

20_____ _____

_____

_____

_____

_____

20_____ _____

_____

_____

_____

_____

If you could have any painting in the world hanging in your house, which one would you want?

30
April

20___ _____

_____

_____

_____

_____

20___ _____

_____

_____

_____

_____

20___ _____

_____

_____

_____

_____

May

When was the last time you forgave yourself
for something?

1
May

20___ _____

_____

_____

_____

_____

20___ _____

_____

_____

_____

_____

20___ _____

_____

_____

_____

_____

2
May

If you could bring one fictional character to life, who would it be?

20___ _____

_____

_____

_____

_____

20___ _____

_____

_____

_____

_____

20___ _____

_____

_____

_____

_____

Where or to whom do you currently go for inspiration?

3
May

20___ _____

_____

_____

_____

_____

20___ _____

_____

_____

_____

_____

20___ _____

_____

_____

_____

_____

4
May

What is something you wish you could change about the past?

20___ _____

_____

_____

_____

_____

20___ _____

_____

_____

_____

_____

20___ _____

_____

_____

_____

_____

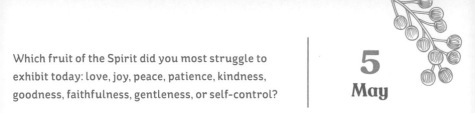

Which fruit of the Spirit did you most struggle to exhibit today: love, joy, peace, patience, kindness, goodness, faithfulness, gentleness, or self-control?

5
May

20___ _____

_____

_____

_____

_____

20___ _____

_____

_____

_____

_____

20___ _____

_____

_____

_____

_____

6
May

If you were to save up for a trip, where would you want to travel?

20_____ _____

_____

_____

_____

_____

20_____ _____

_____

_____

_____

_____

20_____ _____

_____

_____

_____

_____

"My coworkers would describe me as
_____."

7
May

20___ _____

_____

_____

_____

_____

_____

20___ _____

_____

_____

_____

_____

20___ _____

_____

_____

_____

_____

_____

8
May

If you lived in a fictional world and could commit any crime and get away with it, what would your crime be?

20____ _____

_____

_____

_____

_____

20____ _____

_____

_____

_____

_____

20____ _____

_____

_____

_____

_____

What details do you remember about the first time you met your significant other?

9
May

20_____ _____

_____

_____

_____

_____

20_____ _____

_____

_____

_____

_____

20_____ _____

_____

_____

_____

_____

10
May

"I'm proud of how we _____."

20___ _____

20___ _____

20___ _____

What is your current go-to recipe when hosting family or friends?

11
May

20___ _____

_____

_____

_____

_____

_____

20___ _____

_____

_____

_____

_____

_____

20___ _____

_____

_____

_____

_____

_____

12
May

"An upcoming event I'm dreading is
_____."

20___ _____

_____

_____

_____

_____

20___ _____

_____

_____

_____

_____

20___ _____

_____

_____

_____

_____

How can you encourage or support your significant other's hobbies or interests?

13
May

20___ _____

_____

_____

_____

_____

20___ _____

_____

_____

_____

_____

20___ _____

_____

_____

_____

_____

14
May

Describe your current favorite photograph of you and your significant other.

20____ _____

_____

_____

_____

_____

20____ _____

_____

_____

_____

_____

20____ _____

_____

_____

_____

_____

If your life were made into a movie, which actor would probably play you? Who would you want to play you?

15
May

20____ _____

_____

_____

_____

_____

20____ _____

_____

_____

_____

_____

20____ _____

_____

_____

_____

_____

16
May

What is a challenge you have recently overcome?

20____ _____

_____

_____

_____

_____

20____ _____

_____

_____

_____

_____

20____ _____

_____

_____

_____

_____

What quote or song lyric do you think summarizes
your relationship right now?

17
May

20____ _____

_____

_____

_____

_____

20____ _____

_____

_____

_____

_____

20____ _____

_____

_____

_____

_____

18
May

How has your faith evolved over the past year?

20___ _____

_____

_____

_____

_____

20___ _____

_____

_____

_____

_____

20___ _____

_____

_____

_____

_____

What is something you always take with you
on a trip?

19
May

20___

20___

20___

20
May

What was the best and worst thing about today?

20___ _____

_____

_____

_____

_____

20___ _____

_____

_____

_____

_____

20___ _____

_____

_____

_____

_____

Describe an embarrassing event that has happened to you in public.

21
May

20____ _____

_____

_____

_____

_____

20____ _____

_____

_____

_____

_____

20____ _____

_____

_____

_____

_____

22
May

When did you need patience this week?

20___ —————————————————————————

_____

_____

_____

_____

20___ —————————————————————————

_____

_____

_____

_____

20___ —————————————————————————

_____

_____

_____

_____

What is one item you have checked off your bucket
list in the last six months?

23
May

20____ _____

_____

_____

_____

_____

20____ _____

_____

_____

_____

_____

20____ _____

_____

_____

_____

_____

24
May

What is a favorite memory of someone who isn't in your life anymore?

20___ _____

_____

_____

_____

_____

20___ _____

_____

_____

_____

_____

20___ _____

_____

_____

_____

_____

What's an ideal weekend for you?

25
May

20_____ _____

_____

_____

_____

_____

20_____ _____

_____

_____

_____

_____

20_____ _____

_____

_____

_____

_____

26
May

Who was the last friend or family member to stay with you?

20___ _____

_____

_____

_____

_____

20___ _____

_____

_____

_____

_____

20___ _____

_____

_____

_____

_____

What musician or artist has had a great impact on you recently?

27
May

20_____ _____

_____

_____

_____

_____

_____

20_____ _____

_____

_____

_____

_____

_____

20_____ _____

_____

_____

_____

_____

_____

28
May

How have you handled conflict differently this year?

20___ _____

20___ _____

20___ _____

In which fictional world would you most like to live right now?

29
May

20___ _____

_____

_____

_____

_____

20___ _____

_____

_____

_____

_____

20___ _____

_____

_____

_____

_____

30
May

What is your current favorite Scripture verse or inspirational quote?

20_____ _____

_____

_____

_____

_____

20_____ _____

_____

_____

_____

_____

20_____ _____

_____

_____

_____

_____

If you could trade lives with anyone for a day, whom would you choose?

31
May

20____ _____

_____

_____

_____

_____

20____ _____

_____

_____

_____

_____

20____ _____

_____

_____

_____

_____

June

What was one major turning point in your life?

1
June

20___ _____

_____

_____

_____

_____

20___ _____

_____

_____

_____

_____

20___ _____

_____

_____

_____

_____

2
June

What do you like to collect when you travel?

20___ _____

_____

_____

_____

_____

20___ _____

_____

_____

_____

_____

20___ _____

_____

_____

_____

_____

"I don't like it when people _____."

3
June

20___ _____

_____

_____

_____

_____

_____

20___ _____

_____

_____

_____

_____

_____

20___ _____

_____

_____

_____

_____

_____

4
June

Describe a prank someone pulled on you.

20_____ _____

_____

_____

_____

_____

20_____ _____

_____

_____

_____

_____

20_____ _____

_____

_____

_____

_____

What adjective describes how you feel right now?

5
June

20____

_____

_____

_____

_____

_____

20____

_____

_____

_____

_____

_____

20____

_____

_____

_____

_____

_____

6
June

If you had to switch careers, what would you pursue?

20___ _____

_____

_____

_____

_____

_____

20___ _____

_____

_____

_____

_____

_____

20___ _____

_____

_____

_____

_____

_____

Do you have any recurring dreams? Describe one.

7
June

20___ _____

_____

_____

_____

_____

20___ _____

_____

_____

_____

_____

20___ _____

_____

_____

_____

_____

8
June

How important is mentorship to you? Why?

20___ _____

_____

_____

_____

_____

20___ _____

_____

_____

_____

_____

20___ _____

_____

_____

_____

_____

What is a favorite memory about a childhood pet or
another pet in your extended family?

9
June

20___ _____

_____

_____

_____

_____

20___ _____

_____

_____

_____

_____

20___ _____

_____

_____

_____

_____

10
June

What kind of friends do you currently need in your life?

20_____

20_____

20_____

Name one memorable gift you have received from your significant other recently.

11
June

20___ _____

_____

_____

_____

_____

20___ _____

_____

_____

_____

_____

20___ _____

_____

_____

_____

_____

12
June

What new hobby have you been pursuing?

20_____

20_____

20_____

If you could have any artist, living or dead, paint a portrait of you and your significant other, whom would it be?

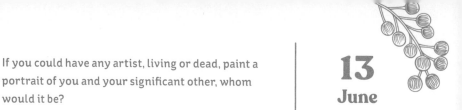

13
June

20____ _____

_____

_____

_____

_____

20____ _____

_____

_____

_____

_____

20____ _____

_____

_____

_____

_____

14
June

What is one of your favorite books that you think your significant other is missing out on?

20____ _____

_____

_____

_____

_____

20____ _____

_____

_____

_____

_____

20____ _____

_____

_____

_____

_____

What helps you alleviate stress?

15
June

20___ _____

_____

_____

_____

_____

_____

20___ _____

_____

_____

_____

_____

_____

20___ _____

_____

_____

_____

_____

_____

16
June

If you had a superpower, what would it be?

20____

20____

20____

Open a Bible or book and put your finger down on a random spot. Which verse or quote did you land on?

17
June

20___ _____

_____

_____

_____

_____

20___ _____

_____

_____

_____

_____

20___ _____

_____

_____

_____

_____

18
June

If you could speak another language, which one would it be?

20___ _____

_____

_____

_____

_____

20___ _____

_____

_____

_____

_____

20___ _____

_____

_____

_____

_____

Which animal do you wish weren't extinct?

19
June

20___ _____

_____

_____

_____

_____

20___ _____

_____

_____

_____

_____

20___ _____

_____

_____

_____

_____

20
June

Who is your current favorite comedian?

20____ _____

_____

_____

_____

_____

20____ _____

_____

_____

_____

_____

20____ _____

_____

_____

_____

_____

Share a funny story about work or a previous job.

21
June

20___ _____

_____

_____

_____

_____

20___ _____

_____

_____

_____

_____

20___ _____

_____

_____

_____

_____

22
June

"One of my favorite things about our home is
_____."

20____ _____

_____

_____

_____

_____

20____ _____

_____

_____

_____

_____

20____ _____

_____

_____

_____

_____

What is your favorite summertime activity?

23
June

20___ _____

_____

_____

_____

_____

20___ _____

_____

_____

_____

_____

20___ _____

_____

_____

_____

_____

24
June

What are some of your hopes for your relationship?

20___ _____

_____

_____

_____

_____

20___ _____

_____

_____

_____

_____

20___ _____

_____

_____

_____

_____

If you could be related to any celebrity, whom would it be?

25
June

20___ _____

_____

_____

_____

_____

20___ _____

_____

_____

_____

_____

20___ _____

_____

_____

_____

_____

26
June

What song have you recently been listening to on repeat?

20_____ _____

_____

_____

_____

_____

_____

20_____ _____

_____

_____

_____

_____

_____

20_____ _____

_____

_____

_____

_____

When was the last time your significant other was a comfort to you?

27
June

20____ _____

_____

_____

_____

_____

20____ _____

_____

_____

_____

_____

20____ _____

_____

_____

_____

_____

28
June

What was the last movie you watched? How did it make you feel?

20____ _____

_____

_____

_____

_____

20____ _____

_____

_____

_____

_____

20____ _____

_____

_____

_____

_____

If you could start a business together, what would it be?

29
June

20____ _____

_____

_____

_____

_____

20____ _____

_____

_____

_____

_____

20____ _____

_____

_____

_____

_____

30
June

How can you and your partner encourage each other this week?

20____ _____

_____

_____

_____

_____

20____ _____

_____

_____

_____

_____

20____ _____

_____

_____

_____

_____

July

1
July

Describe your ideal vacation.

20___ _____

_____

_____

_____

_____

20___ _____

_____

_____

_____

_____

20___ _____

_____

_____

_____

_____

"I am amazed by you when _____."

2
July

20___ _____

_____

_____

_____

_____

_____

20___ _____

_____

_____

_____

_____

_____

20___ _____

_____

_____

_____

_____

_____

3

July

What is one of your favorite inside jokes with your significant other?

20____ _____

_____

_____

_____

_____

20____ _____

_____

_____

_____

_____

20____ _____

_____

_____

_____

_____

What is the last fact you learned about your
country's history?

4
July

20___ _____

_____

_____

_____

_____

20___ _____

_____

_____

_____

_____

20___ _____

_____

_____

_____

_____

5
July

How did you spend the Fourth of July?

20___ _____

_____

_____

_____

_____

20___ _____

_____

_____

_____

_____

20___ _____

_____

_____

_____

_____

What chore do you most appreciate your significant other doing?

6
July

20___ _____

_____

_____

_____

_____

20___ _____

_____

_____

_____

_____

20___ _____

_____

_____

_____

_____

7
July

What's on your to-do list?

20___ _____

_____

_____

_____

_____

20___ _____

_____

_____

_____

_____

20___ _____

_____

_____

_____

_____

What did you do the last time you spent a night out with friends?

8
July

20___ _____

_____

_____

_____

_____

20___ _____

_____

_____

_____

_____

20___ _____

_____

_____

_____

_____

9
July

How have you experienced God's providence recently?

20___ _____

20___ _____

20___ _____

When did you last feel critical of yourself, and for what?

10
July

20____ _____

_____

_____

_____

_____

20____ _____

_____

_____

_____

_____

20____ _____

_____

_____

_____

_____

11
July

What is your current favorite quote from a film?

20___

20___

20___

When was the last time you turned a negative into a positive?

12
July

20___ _____

_____

_____

_____

_____

20___ _____

_____

_____

_____

_____

20___ _____

_____

_____

_____

_____

13
July

If you and your significant other were superheroes, what would your names be?

20____ _____

_____

_____

_____

_____

20____ _____

_____

_____

_____

_____

20____ _____

_____

_____

_____

_____

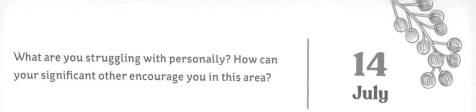

What are you struggling with personally? How can your significant other encourage you in this area?

14
July

20_____ _____

_____

_____

_____

_____

_____

20_____ _____

_____

_____

_____

_____

_____

20_____ _____

_____

_____

_____

_____

_____

15
July

If scientists called you to ask if you would volunteer to live on Mars, how would you respond?

20____ _____

_____

_____

_____

_____

20____ _____

_____

_____

_____

_____

20____ _____

_____

_____

_____

_____

Write down something that happened the last time you went to the beach.

16
July

20___ _____

_____

_____

_____

_____

20___ _____

_____

_____

_____

_____

20___ _____

_____

_____

_____

_____

17
July

How would you like to celebrate your next birthday?

20____ _____

_____

_____

_____

_____

20____ _____

_____

_____

_____

_____

20____ _____

_____

_____

_____

_____

Which board game do you currently hate the most?

18
July

20___ _____

20___ _____

20___ _____

19
July

What story have you recently heard your significant other tell repeatedly?

20____ _____

_____

_____

_____

_____

20____ _____

_____

_____

_____

_____

20____ _____

_____

_____

_____

_____

What is one thing in your relationship that makes you happy right now?

20
July

20___ _____

_____

_____

_____

_____

20___ _____

_____

_____

_____

_____

20___ _____

_____

_____

_____

_____

21
July

"I wish I were better at _____."

20____ _____

_____

_____

_____

_____

_____

20____ _____

_____

_____

_____

_____

_____

20____ _____

_____

_____

_____

_____

_____

What is something you value in a friendship?

22
July

20___

20___

20___

23
July

How do you recover when you're in a bad mood?

20___ —————————————————————————

20___ —————————————————————————

20___ —————————————————————————

What book do you wish you could have written?

24
July

20___ _____

_____

_____

_____

_____

_____

20___ _____

_____

_____

_____

_____

_____

20___ _____

_____

_____

_____

_____

_____

25
July

What behavior or tendency did you inherit from your
parents when it comes to handling conflict?

20___ _____

_____

_____

_____

_____

20___ _____

_____

_____

_____

_____

20___ _____

_____

_____

_____

_____

What is one of you and your partner's greatest strengths as a couple?

26
July

20____ _____

_____

_____

_____

_____

20____ _____

_____

_____

_____

_____

20____ _____

_____

_____

_____

_____

27
July

What is the last devotional or inspirational material you read?

20___ _____

_____

_____

_____

_____

20___ _____

_____

_____

_____

_____

20___ _____

_____

_____

_____

_____

In what ways have you grown in the last year?

28
July

20____ _____

_____

_____

_____

_____

20____ _____

_____

_____

_____

_____

20____ _____

_____

_____

_____

_____

31
July

Describe your significant other's laugh.

20___ _____

_____

_____

_____

_____

_____

20___ _____

_____

_____

_____

_____

_____

20___ _____

_____

_____

_____

_____

August

1
August

What is one way your significant other put your needs first in the previous month?

20___ _____

_____

_____

_____

_____

20___ _____

_____

_____

_____

_____

20___ _____

_____

_____

_____

_____

Recount something funny that happened to you in an airport.

2
August

20___ _____

_____

_____

_____

_____

20___ _____

_____

_____

_____

_____

20___ _____

_____

_____

_____

_____

3
August

"It makes me happy to see you _____."

20___ _____

_____

_____

_____

_____

20___ _____

_____

_____

_____

_____

20___ _____

_____

_____

_____

_____

How do you feel about your career path?

4
August

20___ _____

_____

_____

_____

_____

_____

20___ _____

_____

_____

_____

_____

_____

20___ _____

_____

_____

_____

_____

_____

5
August

Describe a time when you really had to stretch your faith.

20___ _____

_____

_____

_____

_____

20___ _____

_____

_____

_____

_____

20___ _____

_____

_____

_____

_____

What is one way your and your partner's families are alike? Different?

6
August

20___ _____

_____

_____

_____

_____

20___ _____

_____

_____

_____

_____

20___ _____

_____

_____

_____

_____

7
August

What musical instrument do you wish you could play?

20___ _____

_____

_____

_____

_____

20___ _____

_____

_____

_____

_____

20___ _____

_____

_____

_____

_____

What is one regret you have from the past year?

8
August

20___ _____

_____

_____

_____

_____

_____

20___ _____

_____

_____

_____

_____

_____

20___ _____

_____

_____

_____

_____

_____

9
August

What do you need to tell yourself today?

20_____ _____

_____

_____

_____

_____

_____

20_____ _____

_____

_____

_____

_____

_____

20_____ _____

_____

_____

_____

_____

_____

Which movie or TV show do you associate with specific memories of your time together?

10
August

20___ _____

_____

_____

_____

_____

20___ _____

_____

_____

_____

_____

20___ _____

_____

_____

_____

_____

11
August

What do you think is currently keeping you from pursuing a dream?

20___ _____

_____

_____

_____

_____

20___ _____

_____

_____

_____

_____

20___ _____

_____

_____

_____

_____

When do you feel most at peace?

12
August

20_____ _____

_____

_____

_____

_____

20_____ _____

_____

_____

_____

_____

20_____ _____

_____

_____

_____

_____

13
August

What are some budget-friendly weekend trips you could take together?

20___ _____

_____

_____

_____

_____

20___ _____

_____

_____

_____

_____

20___ _____

_____

_____

_____

_____

What is something you're currently obsessed with?

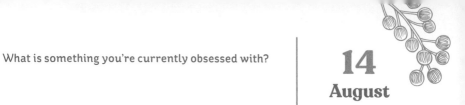

14
August

20____ _____

_____

_____

_____

_____

20____ _____

_____

_____

_____

_____

20____ _____

_____

_____

_____

_____

15
August

Describe your last experience with a thunderstorm.

20___ _____

_____

_____

_____

_____

20___ _____

_____

_____

_____

_____

20___ _____

_____

_____

_____

_____

What was the last item you lost?

20___ _____

_____

_____

_____

_____

20___ _____

_____

_____

_____

_____

20___ _____

_____

_____

_____

_____

17
August

What is the dumbest thing you've ever had a meltdown over?

20____ _____

_____

_____

_____

_____

20____ _____

_____

_____

_____

_____

20____ _____

_____

_____

_____

_____

What personal quality or characteristic are you most proud of?

18
August

20____ _____

_____

_____

_____

_____

20____ _____

_____

_____

_____

_____

20____ _____

_____

_____

_____

_____

19
August

What do you hope retirement will look like for you?

20___ _____

_____

_____

_____

_____

20___ _____

_____

_____

_____

_____

20___ _____

_____

_____

_____

_____

Who comes to mind when you think of a role model
for healthy relationships? Why?

20
August

20_____ _____

_____

_____

_____

_____

_____

20_____ _____

_____

_____

_____

_____

_____

20_____ _____

_____

_____

_____

_____

_____

21
August

Describe a phase you went through when you were a teenager.

20____ _____

_____

_____

_____

_____

20____ _____

_____

_____

_____

_____

20____ _____

_____

_____

_____

_____

What is something new you've recently learned
about your significant other?

22
August

20___ _____

_____

_____

_____

_____

20___ _____

_____

_____

_____

_____

20___ _____

_____

_____

_____

_____

23
August

Paint, pastels, or colored pencils? Why?

20____ _____

_____

_____

_____

_____

20____ _____

_____

_____

_____

_____

20____ _____

_____

_____

_____

_____

What is a friendship deal breaker for you?

24
August

20___ _____

_____

_____

_____

_____

_____

20___ _____

_____

_____

_____

_____

_____

20___ _____

_____

_____

_____

_____

_____

25
August

What is one piece of wisdom you hope to impart to future generations?

20___ _____

_____

_____

_____

_____

20___ _____

_____

_____

_____

_____

20___ _____

_____

_____

_____

_____

If you had to choose only one type of cuisine to eat for the rest of your life, which would it be?

26
August

20____ _____

_____

_____

_____

_____

20____ _____

_____

_____

_____

_____

20____ _____

_____

_____

_____

_____

29
August

What is your current favorite soundtrack?

20____ _____

_____

_____

_____

_____

20____ _____

_____

_____

_____

_____

20____ _____

_____

_____

_____

_____

What is one thing you love about being with your significant other?

30
August

20___ _____

_____

_____

_____

_____

20___ _____

_____

_____

_____

_____

20___ _____

_____

_____

_____

_____

31
August

In what way have you experienced a glimpse of heaven recently?

20____ _____

_____

_____

_____

_____

20____ _____

_____

_____

_____

_____

20____ _____

_____

_____

_____

_____

What do you have trouble believing God can do?

4
September

20_____ _____

_____

_____

_____

_____

20_____ _____

_____

_____

_____

_____

20_____ _____

_____

_____

_____

_____

5
September

"Tomorrow will be a good day to _____."

20___ _____

_____

_____

_____

_____

20___ _____

_____

_____

_____

_____

20___ _____

_____

_____

_____

_____

If you could pick one age to stay forever, which age would you choose?

6
September

20____ _____

_____

_____

_____

_____

20____ _____

_____

_____

_____

_____

20____ _____

_____

_____

_____

_____

7
September

What city currently describes your relationship?

20___ _____

_____

_____

_____

_____

20___ _____

_____

_____

_____

_____

20___ _____

_____

_____

_____

_____

What is a favorite memory you have shared since
you've been together?

8
September

20___ _____

_____

_____

_____

_____

20___ _____

_____

_____

_____

_____

20___ _____

_____

_____

_____

_____

9
September

Whom do you currently talk to when you need advice?

20___ _____

_____

_____

_____

_____

20___ _____

_____

_____

_____

_____

20___ _____

_____

_____

_____

_____

With which family member did you last share a
phone call? What did you talk about?

10
September

20___ _____

_____

_____

_____

_____

20___ _____

_____

_____

_____

_____

20___ _____

_____

_____

_____

_____

11
September

When were you last in a house of worship?
Why were you there?

20____ _____

20____ _____

20____ _____

What is a book you wish would be made
into a movie?

12
September

20___ _____

_____

_____

_____

_____

20___ _____

_____

_____

_____

_____

20___ _____

_____

_____

_____

_____

13
September

Describe a time when you struggled in your relationship. How did you get through it?

20____ _____

_____

_____

_____

_____

20____ _____

_____

_____

_____

_____

20____ _____

_____

_____

_____

_____

Would you rather look at art or create it?

14
September

20___ _____

_____

_____

_____

_____

20___ _____

_____

_____

_____

_____

20___ _____

_____

_____

_____

_____

15
September

If you could discover any magical creature, what would it be?

20___ _____

_____

_____

_____

_____

20___ _____

_____

_____

_____

_____

20___ _____

_____

_____

_____

_____

When do you feel the most "you"?

16
September

20___ _____

_____

_____

_____

_____

20___ _____

_____

_____

_____

_____

20___ _____

_____

_____

_____

_____

17
September

Where can you volunteer locally this year?

20___ _____

_____

_____

_____

_____

_____

20___ _____

_____

_____

_____

_____

_____

20___ _____

_____

_____

_____

_____

_____

What Bible story inspires you?

18
September

20___ _____

_____

_____

_____

_____

_____

20___ _____

_____

_____

_____

_____

_____

20___ _____

_____

_____

_____

_____

_____

19
September

What is the top item on your Christmas wish list this year?

20___ _____

_____

_____

_____

_____

20___ _____

_____

_____

_____

_____

20___ _____

_____

_____

_____

_____

"Something that bores me is _____."

20
September

20____ _____

_____

_____

_____

_____

20____ _____

_____

_____

_____

_____

20____ _____

_____

_____

_____

_____

21
September

Who is your favorite movie star or celebrity?

20___ _____

_____

_____

_____

_____

20___ _____

_____

_____

_____

_____

20___ _____

_____

_____

_____

_____

What is a similarity between you and your partner's relationship and your parents' relationship?

22
September

20____ _____

_____

_____

_____

_____

20____ _____

_____

_____

_____

_____

20____ _____

_____

_____

_____

_____

23
September

What are your hopes for this fall?

20____ _____

_____

_____

_____

_____

20____ _____

_____

_____

_____

_____

20____ _____

_____

_____

_____

_____

What was the last gag gift you received?

24
September

20____ _____

_____

_____

_____

_____

20____ _____

_____

_____

_____

_____

20____ _____

_____

_____

_____

_____

25
September

Do you prefer photographs or paintings? Why?

20___ _____

_____

_____

_____

_____

_____

20___ _____

_____

_____

_____

_____

_____

20___ _____

_____

_____

_____

_____

_____

What book inspired you as a child?

26
September

20____ _____

_____

_____

_____

_____

20____ _____

_____

_____

_____

_____

20____ _____

_____

_____

_____

_____

27
September

What is a tendency you fall back on when responding to hardship?

20____ _____

_____

_____

_____

_____

20____ _____

_____

_____

_____

_____

20____ _____

_____

_____

_____

_____

Which movie genre is your current favorite?

28
September

20____ _____

_____

_____

_____

_____

20____ _____

_____

_____

_____

_____

20____ _____

_____

_____

_____

_____

29
September

In what ways have you recently been intentional about strengthening your relationship?

20____ _____

_____

_____

_____

_____

20____ _____

_____

_____

_____

_____

20____ _____

_____

_____

_____

_____

If you were independently wealthy, what would you spend your time doing?

30
September

20___ _____

_____

_____

_____

_____

20___ _____

_____

_____

_____

_____

20___ _____

_____

_____

_____

_____

October

If you could easily memorize an entire book of the Bible or a chapter in a book, which would it be?

1
October

20_____

20_____

20_____

2
October

What is one of your most prized souvenirs?

20_____ _____

_____

_____

_____

_____

_____

20_____ _____

_____

_____

_____

_____

_____

20_____ _____

_____

_____

_____

_____

_____

Have you ever witnessed a miracle (literally or figuratively)?

3
October

20___ _____

_____

_____

_____

_____

_____

20___ _____

_____

_____

_____

_____

_____

20___ _____

_____

_____

_____

_____

_____

4
October

What do you feel grateful for today?

20___ _____

_____

_____

_____

_____

20___ _____

_____

_____

_____

_____

20___ _____

_____

_____

_____

_____

What type of humor annoys you at this point
in your life?

5
October

20____ _____

_____

_____

_____

_____

20____ _____

_____

_____

_____

_____

20____ _____

_____

_____

_____

_____

6
October

What is the weirdest thing that has happened to you this year?

20____ _____

_____

_____

_____

_____

20____ _____

_____

_____

_____

_____

20____ _____

_____

_____

_____

_____

What comforts you?

7
October

20___ _____

20___ _____

20___ _____

8
October

"This weekend I want to _____."

20___ _____

_____

_____

_____

_____

_____

20___ _____

_____

_____

_____

_____

_____

20___ _____

_____

_____

_____

_____

_____

What is a story you've never told your significant
other about growing up in your family?

9
October

20___ _____

_____

_____

_____

_____

_____

20___ _____

_____

_____

_____

_____

_____

20___ _____

_____

_____

_____

_____

_____

10
October

If you could gain the skill of any one particular artist, whom would it be?

20_____ _____

_____

_____

_____

_____

_____

20_____ _____

_____

_____

_____

_____

20_____ _____

_____

_____

_____

_____

If you could take a year off and do whatever you wanted, what would you do?

11
October

20___ _____

_____

_____

_____

_____

20___ _____

_____

_____

_____

_____

20___ _____

_____

_____

_____

_____

12
October

What book would you like to read with your
significant other?

20___ _____

_____

_____

_____

_____

20___ _____

_____

_____

_____

_____

20___ _____

_____

_____

_____

_____

What do you struggle with the most in the way you view yourself?

13
October

20___ _____

_____

_____

_____

_____

20___ _____

_____

_____

_____

_____

20___ _____

_____

_____

_____

_____

14
October

In the past year, how did you study the Bible?

20___ _____

_____

_____

_____

_____

_____

20___ _____

_____

_____

_____

_____

_____

20___ _____

_____

_____

_____

_____

What is something you remember about your early travels together?

15
October

20___ _____

_____

_____

_____

_____

20___ _____

_____

_____

_____

_____

20___ _____

_____

_____

_____

_____

16
October

What superhero inspires you the most?

20___ _____

20___ _____

20___ _____

"I love it when my significant other _____."

17
October

20___ _____

_____

_____

_____

_____

_____

20___ _____

_____

_____

_____

_____

_____

20___ _____

_____

_____

_____

_____

_____

18
October

Do you celebrate Halloween? If so, what costume are you planning to wear this year?

20___ _____

_____

_____

_____

_____

20___ _____

_____

_____

_____

_____

20___ _____

_____

_____

_____

_____

Given another opportunity, what situation would you have handled differently?

19
October

20___ _____

_____

_____

_____

_____

20___ _____

_____

_____

_____

_____

20___ _____

_____

_____

_____

_____

20
October

What TV or movie theme song would you say reflects your life?

20____ _____

_____

_____

_____

_____

20____ _____

_____

_____

_____

_____

20____ _____

_____

_____

_____

_____

What did you do last week to ensure that your significant other's needs and wants were met?

21
October

20___ _____

_____

_____

_____

_____

20___ _____

_____

_____

_____

_____

20___ _____

_____

_____

_____

_____

22
October

Who was the last friend or family member you visited as a couple?

20____ _____

_____

_____

_____

_____

20____ _____

_____

_____

_____

_____

20____ _____

_____

_____

_____

_____

If you pray as a couple, what do you pray about?

23
October

20___ _____

_____

_____

_____

_____

_____

20___ _____

_____

_____

_____

_____

_____

20___ _____

_____

_____

_____

_____

24
October

What are you currently reading for fun?

20____ _____

_____

_____

_____

_____

_____

20____ _____

_____

_____

_____

_____

_____

20____ _____

_____

_____

_____

_____

_____

How do you handle grief?

25
October

20___ _____

_____

_____

_____

_____

20___ _____

_____

_____

_____

_____

20___ _____

_____

_____

_____

_____

26
October

If you were to describe yourself using a movie genre, which one would you choose?

20_____

20_____

20_____

What do you consider to be your spiritual gift(s)?

27
October

20___ _____

_____

_____

_____

_____

20___ _____

_____

_____

_____

_____

20___ _____

_____

_____

_____

_____

28
October

In seasons of busyness, how do you and your significant other take care of each other?

20_____ _____

20_____ _____

20_____ _____

What brings you the most joy?

29
October

20___ _____
_____
_____
_____
_____

20___ _____
_____
_____
_____
_____

20___ _____
_____
_____
_____
_____

30
October

If you could meet your favorite literary character, whom would it be?

20____ _____

_____

_____

_____

_____

20____ _____

_____

_____

_____

_____

20____ _____

_____

_____

_____

_____

What is a favorite fall tradition of yours?

31
October

20___ _____

_____

_____

_____

_____

20___ _____

_____

_____

_____

_____

20___ _____

_____

_____

_____

_____

November

What brings you the most satisfaction in your everyday life?

1
November

20___ _____

_____

_____

_____

_____

20___ _____

_____

_____

_____

_____

20___ _____

_____

_____

_____

_____

2
November

What is it about your family that you are most thankful for?

20___ _____

_____

_____

_____

_____

20___ _____

_____

_____

_____

_____

20___ _____

_____

_____

_____

_____

If you wrote a memoir about your life, what would the title be?

3
November

20___ _____

_____

_____

_____

_____

20___ _____

_____

_____

_____

_____

20___ _____

_____

_____

_____

_____

4
November

How did you react the last time you heard bad news?

20___ _____

_____

_____

_____

_____

_____

20___ _____

_____

_____

_____

_____

_____

20___ _____

_____

_____

_____

_____

_____

How has your faith been challenged recently?

5
November

20___ _____

_____

_____

_____

_____

20___ _____

_____

_____

_____

_____

20___ _____

_____

_____

_____

_____

6
November

If you could live anywhere else in the world, where would it be?

20____ _____

_____

_____

_____

_____

20____ _____

_____

_____

_____

_____

20____ _____

_____

_____

_____

_____

"I'm getting better at _____."

7
November

20___ _____

_____

_____

_____

_____

_____

20___ _____

_____

_____

_____

_____

_____

20___ _____

_____

_____

_____

_____

8
November

Where are you planning to spend Thanksgiving this year?

20____ _____

_____

_____

_____

_____

20____ _____

_____

_____

_____

_____

20____ _____

_____

_____

_____

_____

What is your typical Sunday/Sabbath routine?

9
November

20___ _____

_____

_____

_____

_____

20___ _____

_____

_____

_____

_____

20___ _____

_____

_____

_____

_____

10
November

What is one prank you would love to try?

20____ _____

_____

_____

_____

_____

20____ _____

_____

_____

_____

_____

20____ _____

_____

_____

_____

_____

What are you looking forward to?

11
November

20___ _____

_____

_____

_____

_____

20___ _____

_____

_____

_____

_____

20___ _____

_____

_____

_____

_____

12
November

What is one of your current pet peeves other people do in daily life?

20_____

20_____

20_____

How have you documented your memories over the past year?

13
November

20___ _____

_____

_____

_____

_____

20___ _____

_____

_____

_____

_____

20___ _____

_____

_____

_____

_____

14
November

Describe your favorite scene from a movie you watched together recently.

20___ _____

_____

_____

_____

_____

20___ _____

_____

_____

_____

_____

20___ _____

_____

_____

_____

_____

What are you worrying about?

15
November

20___ _____

_____

_____

_____

_____

20___ _____

_____

_____

_____

_____

20___ _____

_____

_____

_____

_____

16
November

What's the last thing you read that really spoke to you?

20_____

_____

_____

_____

_____

_____

20_____

_____

_____

_____

_____

_____

20_____

_____

_____

_____

_____

_____

What is your favorite Bible verse?

17
November

20____ _____

_____

_____

_____

_____

20____ _____

_____

_____

_____

_____

20____ _____

_____

_____

_____

_____

18
November

If you went on a trip together to help others, where would you go?

20___ _____

_____

_____

_____

_____

20___ _____

_____

_____

_____

_____

20___ _____

_____

_____

_____

_____

What did your significant other do recently that you appreciate?

19
November

20_____ _____

_____

_____

_____

_____

20_____ _____

_____

_____

_____

_____

20_____ _____

_____

_____

_____

_____

20
November

How many pets is too many?

20_____ _____

_____

_____

_____

_____

_____

20_____ _____

_____

_____

_____

_____

20_____ _____

_____

_____

_____

_____

Describe your sense of humor.

21
November

20___ _____

_____

_____

_____

_____

_____

20___ _____

_____

_____

_____

_____

_____

20___ _____

_____

_____

_____

_____

_____

22
November

What is something you're thankful for but tend to take for granted?

20___ _____

_____

_____

_____

_____

20___ _____

_____

_____

_____

_____

20___ _____

_____

_____

_____

_____

In what ways can you and your significant other rely on each other when things get hard?

23
November

20___ _____

_____

_____

_____

_____

20___ _____

_____

_____

_____

_____

20___ _____

_____

_____

_____

_____

24
November

Which fruits of the Spirit were you able to exhibit today: love, joy, peace, patience, kindness, goodness, faithfulness, gentleness, or self-control?

20___ _____

_____

_____

_____

_____

20___ _____

_____

_____

_____

_____

20___ _____

_____

_____

_____

_____

Would you rather relax or be on the go the whole time during your next vacation?

25
November

20__ _____

_____

_____

_____

_____

20__ _____

_____

_____

_____

_____

20__ _____

_____

_____

_____

_____

26
November

Why do you (or don't you) go to church?

20___ _____

20___ _____

20___ _____

Which movie or show is your go-to comedy right now?

27
November

20_____ _____

_____

_____

_____

_____

20_____ _____

_____

_____

_____

_____

20_____ _____

_____

_____

_____

_____

28
November

What is your best nonphysical attribute?

20____

20____

20____

When was the last time you felt proud of yourself, and what was it for?

29
November

20_____ _____

_____

_____

_____

_____

20_____ _____

_____

_____

_____

_____

20_____ _____

_____

_____

_____

_____

30
November

What was the best thing about Thanksgiving this year?

20___ _____

_____

_____

_____

_____

20___ _____

_____

_____

_____

_____

20___ _____

_____

_____

_____

_____

December

1
December

What are you most looking forward to over the holidays?

20___ _____

_____

_____

_____

_____

20___ _____

_____

_____

_____

_____

20___ _____

_____

_____

_____

_____

How do you experience peace in this season?

2
December

20___ _____

_____

_____

_____

_____

_____

20___ _____

_____

_____

_____

_____

_____

20___ _____

_____

_____

_____

_____

_____

3

December

What book inspired you when you were a teenager?

20____ _____

_____

_____

_____

_____

20____ _____

_____

_____

_____

_____

20____ _____

_____

_____

_____

_____

Describe a memorable or funny experience
with snow.

4
December

20___ _____

_____

_____

_____

_____

20___ _____

_____

_____

_____

_____

20___ _____

_____

_____

_____

_____

5
December

What's the last movie that made you cry?

20___ _____

_____

_____

_____

_____

20___ _____

_____

_____

_____

_____

20___ _____

_____

_____

_____

_____

When in the past year did you feel closest to God?

6
December

20___ _____

_____

_____

_____

_____

20___ _____

_____

_____

_____

_____

20___ _____

_____

_____

_____

_____

7
December

What did you most enjoy about traveling together in the past year?

20____ _____

_____

_____

_____

_____

_____

20____ _____

_____

_____

_____

_____

_____

20____ _____

_____

_____

_____

_____

_____

Describe a holiday tradition that is unique to your family.

8
December

20___ _____

_____

_____

_____

_____

20___ _____

_____

_____

_____

_____

20___ _____

_____

_____

_____

_____

9
December

Describe a time when your prayers were answered.

20____ _____

_____

_____

_____

_____

20____ _____

_____

_____

_____

_____

20____ _____

_____

_____

_____

_____

What is your favorite time of day?

10
December

20___ _____

_____

_____

_____

_____

20___ _____

_____

_____

_____

_____

20___ _____

_____

_____

_____

_____

11
December

"It still surprises me that _____."

20___ _____

_____

_____

_____

_____

_____

20___ _____

_____

_____

_____

_____

_____

20___ _____

_____

_____

_____

_____

What's the most valuable thing you own?

12
December

20____ _____

20____ _____

20____ _____

13
December

What holiday tradition have you adopted from your significant other's family?

20___ _____

_____

_____

_____

_____

20___ _____

_____

_____

_____

_____

20___ _____

_____

_____

_____

_____

Who could you surprise with a card or small gift
this Christmas?

14
December

20____ _____

_____

_____

_____

_____

_____

20____ _____

_____

_____

_____

_____

_____

20____ _____

_____

_____

_____

_____

_____

15
December

What holiday song are you already sick of hearing?

20___ _____

_____

_____

_____

_____

20___ _____

_____

_____

_____

_____

20___ _____

_____

_____

_____

_____

How have you helped another person recently?

16
December

20___ _____

_____

_____

_____

_____

20___ _____

_____

_____

_____

_____

20___ _____

_____

_____

_____

_____

17
December

What is something you are eager to just "get over with"?

20___ _____

_____

_____

_____

_____

20___ _____

_____

_____

_____

_____

20___ _____

_____

_____

_____

_____

Which fictional couples do you think would be
friends with you?

18
December

20___ _____

_____

_____

_____

_____

20___ _____

_____

_____

_____

_____

20___ _____

_____

_____

_____

_____

19
December

What's your go-to holiday movie this year?

20___ _____

_____

_____

_____

_____

20___ _____

_____

_____

_____

_____

20___ _____

_____

_____

_____

_____

What is a new tradition you and your significant other have created?

20
December

20____ —

20____ —

20____ —

21
December

What are the first words that come to mind when you think of God?

20___ _____

_____

_____

_____

_____

20___ _____

_____

_____

_____

_____

20___ _____

_____

_____

_____

_____

What is a holiday memory from the past that makes you smile?

22
December

20___ _____

_____

_____

_____

_____

_____

20___ _____

_____

_____

_____

_____

_____

20___ _____

_____

_____

_____

_____

_____

23
December

What recent situation required you to exercise patience?

20____ _____

_____

_____

_____

_____

20____ _____

_____

_____

_____

_____

20____ _____

_____

_____

_____

_____

"My favorite thing about this Christmas is
_____."

24
December

20___ _____

_____

_____

_____

_____

20___ _____

_____

_____

_____

_____

20___ _____

_____

_____

_____

_____

25
December

What happened today that you want to remember?

20___ _____

20___ _____

20___ _____

What was the most unexpected, thoughtful, or humorous gift you received this year?

26
December

20____ _____

_____

_____

_____

_____

20____ _____

_____

_____

_____

_____

20____ _____

_____

_____

_____

_____

27
December

What have you accomplished this past year that you are most proud of?

20____ _____

_____

_____

_____

_____

_____

20____ _____

_____

_____

_____

_____

_____

20____ _____

_____

_____

_____

_____

_____

What happened this year that you weren't
expecting?

28
December

20___ _____

_____

_____

_____

_____

20___ _____

_____

_____

_____

_____

20___ _____

_____

_____

_____

_____

29
December

What is your biggest hope for next year?

20____

_____

_____

_____

_____

_____

20____

_____

_____

_____

_____

_____

20____

_____

_____

_____

_____

_____

What was the most surprising thing you learned about your significant other while filling out this book this year?

30
December

20_____ _____

_____

_____

_____

_____

20_____ _____

_____

_____

_____

_____

20_____ _____

_____

_____

_____

_____

31
December

What was the most surprising thing you learned about yourself while filling out this book this year?

20___ _____

_____

_____

_____

_____

20___ _____

_____

_____

_____

_____

20___ _____

_____

_____

_____

_____